BREADFRUIT
PRODUCTION
GUIDE

RECOMMENDED
PRACTICES
FOR GROWING,
HARVESTING,
AND HANDLING

2nd Edition

By Craig Elevitch, Diane Ragone, and Ian Cole

Breadfruit Production Guide: Recommended practices for growing, harvesting, and handling

By Craig Elevitch, Diane Ragone, and Ian Cole

ISBN: 978-1939618030

This is a publication of Hoʻoulu ka ʻUlu—Revitalizing Breadfruit, a project of Hawaiʻi Homegrown Food Network and Breadfruit Institute of the National Tropical Botanical Garden. The Hoʻoulu ka ʻUlu project is directed by Andrea Dean, Craig Elevitch, and Diane Ragone.

Recommended citation

Elevitch, C., D. Ragone, and I. Cole. 2014. Breadfruit Production Guide: Recommended practices for growing, harvesting, and handling (2nd Edition). Breadfruit Institute of the National Tropical Botanical Garden, Kalaheo, Hawaiʻi and Hawaiʻi Homegrown Food Network, Holualoa, Hawaiʻi. www.breadfruit.org and www.breadfruit.info

Sponsor

This publication was produced with funds from the State of Hawaiʻi Department of Agriculture.

Disclaimer

Reasonable efforts have been made to publish reliable information. The authors, editors, and publisher cannot assume responsibility for the validity of all materials or for the consequences of their use. The authors, editors, and publisher shall have neither liability nor responsibility to any person or entity with respect to any loss or damage caused, or alleged to have been caused, directly or indirectly, by the information contained in this publication.

Publishers

Breadfruit Institute
National Tropical Botanical Garden
3530 Papalina Road
Kalaheo, Kauai, Hawaii USA 96741
Email: breadfruitinstitute@ntbg.org
Web: www.breadfruit.org

Hawaiʻi Homegrown Food Network
P.O. Box 5
Holualoa, Hawaii USA 96725
Email: hooulu@hawaiihomegrown.net
Web: www.breadfruit.info, www.hawaiihomegrown.net

Acknowledgments

We are indebted to the many reviewers of this work, who contributed numerous corrections and suggestions that shaped the final publication: Failautusi Avegalio, Jr., Heidi Bornhorst, John Cadman, Jesus Castro, Jim Currie, Andrea Dean, Emihner Johnson, Shirley Kauhaihao, Robert Paull, Grant Percival, the Pacific Breadfruit Project (Andrew McGregor, Livai Tora, Kyle Stice, and Kaitu Erasito), and the Scientific Research Organisation of Samoa (Tilafono David Hunter, Kenneth Wong, Gaufa Salesa Fetu, Kuinimeri Asora Finau). The authors gratefully acknowledge Andrea Dean for input in formulating the content of this guide. Photo contributions by Jim Wiseman, Ric Rocker, and Kamaui Aiona, are greatly appreciated. The kapa ʻulu artwork pictured on cover was crafted by Kumu Wesley Sen. Finally, our deepest gratitude to all of the Pacific Island farmers who have contributed to the knowledge base for breadfruit for generations.

Author bios

Craig Elevitch has been an educator in agroforestry and sustainable human agroecosystems since 1991. He directs Agroforestry Net, a nonprofit educational organization dedicated to empowering people in agroforestry. The organization's internationally recognized publications and workshops have guided thousands in becoming more proficient in ecological food production, agroforestry, and reforestation. Craig's books include *Agroforestry Guides for Pacific Islands* (2000), *Traditional Trees of Pacific Islands: Their Culture, Environment, and Use* (2006), and *Specialty Crops for Pacific Islands* (2011), all of which promote diverse agricultural systems that produce abundant food, fiber, medicine, and other important resources.

Dr. Diane Ragone is Director of the Breadfruit Institute, created in 2003 to promote the conservation and use of breadfruit for food and reforestation. She is an authority on the conservation and use of breadfruit. Her horticultural and ethnobotanical studies on this traditional Pacific crop for 30 years resulted in the establishment of the world's largest collection of breadfruit at the National Tropical Botanical Garden. Dr. Ragone is an Adjunct Professor at the University of Hawaiʻi in the Department of Tropical Plant and Soil Sciences and received a MS and PhD in Horticulture from UH. She is an author of 90 publications on breadfruit, ethnobotany, horticulture, and native plant conservation.

Ian Cole is Collection Manager & Curator at the Breadfruit Institute. He received a BS in Horticulture from the University of Florida and a MS in Environmental Science from the University of British Columbia, Okanagan, Canada. Ian has broad-based training, experience, and expertise in commercial and public garden horticulture, and is a Certified Arborist. Ian manages arboricultural and horticultural operations related to the breadfruit collection, and has extensive experience in the proper planting and care of breadfruit trees, using integrated management practices. Ian has given numerous workshops, lectures, and demonstrations on growing and using breadfruit and published several peer-reviewed and general articles.

CONTENTS

PREFACE

The idea for the *Breadfruit Production Guide* has been germinating for several years and it is exciting to see it in print! Since its inception in 2003, the Breadfruit Institute at the National Tropical Botanical Garden has been promoting the conservation and use of breadfruit for food and reforestation. One of our major projects has involved extensive research on developing micropropagation (tissue culture) methods to propagate breadfruit trees so that more trees could be made available and planted in Hawai'i and elsewhere. Since 2009, more than 10,000 trees of the Ma'afala variety have been planted in yards and farms and communities throughout Hawai'i. In 2013–2014 the Institute will distribute more than 7,000 trees through our "Plant a Tree of Life—Grow 'Ulu" project.

Since the advent of European-style plantation agriculture in the 1800s, populations of breadfruit trees in Hawai'i have steadily declined to a small percentage of their former numbers—until recently. We are currently experiencing the greatest expansion of breadfruit tree plantings in Hawai'i in centuries—and we expect to see thousands more trees planted in upcoming years. We also see an increased interest in caring for, and using the fruit from, the remaining established trees throughout the archipelago. In many areas, these trees are the offspring of groves of the traditional Hawaiian 'Ulu variety planted centuries ago. The production of tens to hundreds of thousands of tons of this nutritious, delicious starchy staple crop has great potential to help provide long-term food and economic security and agricultural sustainability for our state. Breadfruit trees also can also help mitigate climate change effects when planted on open lands by storing carbon and reducing the amount of fuel consuming in shipping food to Hawai'i.

In 2010, the Hawai'i Homegrown Food Network and the Breadfruit Institute launched the Ho'oulu ka 'Ulu project to revitalize breadfruit in Hawai'i. Outreach programs such as festivals, workshops, cooking demonstrations, etc., directly engaged thousands of residents and visitors. It quickly became clear that there is great enthusiasm for breadfruit—planting more trees, utilizing fruit from existing trees, developing value-added products, having fruit available in markets, and seeing breadfruit dishes served in restaurants. However, many people have questions about the basics: What are the different stages of fruit maturity and how can you tell when a fruit is ready to pick or eat? What's the best way to handle a fruit that you harvest or purchase? What's the best and safest way to harvest fruit? This guide is designed to answer these questions and to help the producer, retailer, chef, and consumer obtain the best quality fruit.

This guide is important because it is a practical, extensively illustrated primer to growing, harvesting, and handling breadfruit. It synthesizes and presents information published in the scientific literature as well as practical, hands-on knowledge and expertise gained from working with breadfruit for many years.

Future Directions

For the first time in the long history of breadfruit cultivation and use, it is now possible to propagate large quantities of good quality, uniform planting material. This means that field plantings can be established and basic agronomic questions about tree establishment, management, and care can be answered in a scientific and quantifiable way. What is the best spacing? What are the yields? What are the best methods and crops to interplant? What are the best ways to establish and manage trees? What are the environmental requirements? Are there drought tolerant or cold tolerant varieties? What's the best way to prune and manage young trees? What are the fertilizer needs? What pests and diseases are significant? The answers to these questions and others will benefit home gardeners and farmers to help revitalize breadfruit.

At the same time, the culinary aspects of the fruit and value-added products can now be explored and developed. As just one example, there is currently considerable interest in breadfruit flour: the most efficient and economical ways to process the fruit into flour, its shelf life, appropriate products made from the flour, etc.

I have been working with and learning about breadfruit since 1983. It has been a great privilege, honor, and pleasure to work with the people and breadfruit of more than 50 Pacific islands. I've seen and experienced first hand the importance and value of breadfruit to island societies and environments. I am so grateful to the many agricultural extension agents, farmers, families, and other islanders who welcomed me and gladly shared their knowledge about this amazing tree. Jim Wiseman has been a steadfast supporter and participant in recording this work through photographs and video.

The Hoʻoulu ka ʻUlu project has brought together a diverse network of individuals and organizations in this endeavor to revitalize ʻulu in Hawaiʻi. I have learned so much from my co-authors, Ian Cole and Craig Elevitch, and Andrea Dean, co-director of the Hoʻoulu ka ʻUlu project. I am enthralled with each and every cultural practitioner, culinary artist, and presenter who has participated in our outreach programs. I also appreciate the many who have shared their fruit, recipes, and experiences with breadfruit. All of you have enriched the project in some way, and your contributions have been encapsulated into this guide. What an exhilarating time for breadfruit farmers, researchers, entrepreneurs, chefs, and consumers!

Diane Ragone
Kalaheo, Kauaʻi, Hawaiʻi
February 1, 2014

INTRODUCTION

Breadfruit has long been an important staple crop and a primary component of traditional agroforestry systems in the Pacific, where numerous varieties are grown. Breadfruit was first domesticated in the western Pacific and spread by humans throughout the region over the past 3,000–4,000 years. From Melanesia to Micronesia to Polynesia, many islanders grow and use breadfruit as part of their daily diet. Breadfruit has a significant and often unappreciated legacy in Hawai'i. It is one of the canoe plants brought from the Society Islands centuries ago, and the variety they brought, known simply as 'Ulu (same as the Hawaiian word for breadfruit), was widely grown throughout the archipelago.

There were vast groves on Hawai'i Island in the Kona and Puna districts, with many trees in Hilo and the valleys along the Hāmākua coast and Kohala. There were large groves on Kaua'i along the leeward coasts and windward valleys. On O'ahu, the trees grew mostly on the leeward side in Wailupe, Waikīkī, Kalihi, and 'Ewa, and in sheltered places on the north shore and windward coast. The southern shores of west Maui from Olowalu to Waiehu and east Maui were major areas for 'ulu. On Moloka'i the trees grew mainly on the southern side towards the eastern end of the island. 'Ulu was even abundant on Lāna'i. Beginning in the late 1800s, other varieties were brought to Hawai'i from Micronesia, Samoa, Tonga, Tahiti, and the Philippines, and can be found today in many yards and farms.

Breadfruit varieties introduced into Hawai'i since the late 1800s

Variety	Region of origin	Botanical name
Ma'afala	Samoa	*Artocarpus altilis*
Puou	Samoa/Tonga	*A. altilis*
Maopo	Samoa/Tonga	*A. altilis*
Puero	Tahiti	*A. altilis*
Dugdug	N. Marianas	*A. mariannensis*
Breadnut	Philippines	*A. camansi*
Meinpadahk, Mejenwe	Micronesia	*A. altilis* × *A. mariannensis*

For variety information on characteristics for identification and use, visit www.breadfruit.org.

Why breadfruit has become important in Hawai'i today

'Ulu made significant contributions to food security and agricultural sustainability in the Hawaiian Islands for centuries by providing a long-lived, easy to grow, productive, nutritious, starchy staple crop. Over the past century, breadfruit cultivation and use declined, and many trees were cut down, especially in urban areas over the past 30 to 40 years. The removal of breadfruit trees in most areas came at the same time as food preferences changed, and com-

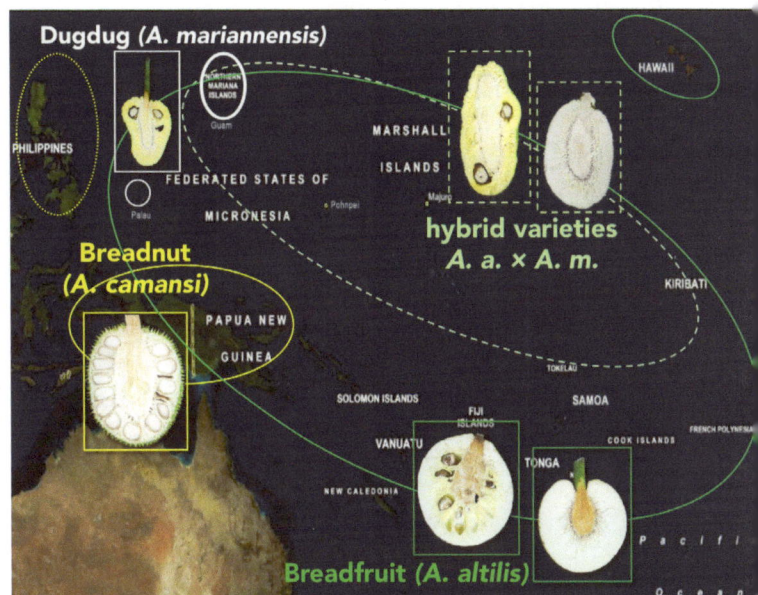

Top: Historical distribution of the breadfruit complex: *Artocarpus altilis*, *A. camansi*, *A. mariannensis*, and *A. altilis* × *A. mariannensis* hybrids. Bottom: The ancient breadfruit region of Kona, Hawai'i, called the kaluulu, was about 29 km (18 mi) long and 1 km (0.6 mi) wide. In this image the estimated location of the kaluulu is depicted in yellow based on the work of Lincoln (2012). Base map: Google Earth.

mon knowledge of how to harvest, select, and prepare breadfruit dishes gradually decreased. In recent years, the supply has been variable and many are unsure about how to grow and harvest high quality breadfruit. This manual is designed to address those concerns.

There is an increasing demand for fresh breadfruit in Hawai'i by residents interested in a traditional island diet for health or cultural reasons. Fresh breadfruit is generally available at local farmers markets and certain grocery stores. More island chefs are beginning to feature or use breadfruit at their restaurants. The U.S. mainland and Canada are potential markets for fresh and processed breadfruit products especially by populations of Pacific and Caribbean islanders who want a taste of home. Breadfruit also shows promise for use in the rapidly growing market for gluten-free foods.

Food security

Today Hawai'i is experiencing a renaissance for breadfruit and other traditional crops that sustained Pacific Islanders for millennia. This has coincided with increased awareness about the critical need for food self-sufficiency and improved health and nutrition. Hawai'i imports about 85% of its food, making it one of the most import-dependent states in the nation. In 2011–2012, more than 14% of Hawai'i residents—183,500 people—were food insecure and received emergency food assistance through the Hawaii Foodbank network (Hawaii Foodbank 2012).

Hawaiians and other Pacific Islanders such as Micronesians, Samoans, and Tongans comprise 10% of the state's population (135,422 people), and 19% live at the poverty level compared to 12% for the general population (Department of Commerce 2010, Macartney et al 2013, and U.S. Census Bureau). These groups are especially vulnerable to food insecurity and health issues, such as obesity and diabetes, associated with a non-traditional diet.

Breadfruit can easily be grown and managed as a backyard tree and interplanted with a wide range of plants (e.g., bananas, taro, citrus, vegetables, etc.), on farms and even in a small yard. Growing breadfruit trees in rural, urban, and community landscapes

© Diane Ragone

© Jim Wiseman

Only by providing quality fruit will markets for breadfruit expand to supermarkets, restaurants, and value-added processors. Left: Breadfruit can commonly be found at farmers markets in Hawai'i that sell local produce, however, it has frequently been harvested at an immature stage, which has inferior eating qualities for most dishes. Right: Soaking fruit immediately after harvest in cold water can extend shelf life while removing debris.

will provide long-term environmental benefits and help sequester atmospheric carbon dioxide. The trees require little attention or care, producing an abundance of food with minimal input of labor or materials. The trees are emblematic of the special connection between Hawai'i's diverse cultures and the environment, the land and its people. A single tree, producing just 100 fruit per year, will provide about 100 kg (220 lbs) or more of food.

Improving diet

The nutritious fruit is an energy-rich food, high in complex carbohydrates and rich in dietary fiber, iron, calcium, potassium, magnesium, thiamin, and niacin. Some varieties are good sources of antioxidants and carotenoids. In Hawai'i, as elsewhere in the Pacific, white rice is the preferred staple starch for reasons of convenience and habit. White rice is a poorer source of many nutrients, such as fiber, potassium, Vitamin C and Vitamin A, and must be imported, while breadfruit is locally grown. Breadfruit is gluten free, and its flour can serve as a replacement for wheat in many recipes and food products that are associated with food allergies and celiac disease. Breadfruit also has a moderate glycemic index, especially when boiled or steamed, compared to potatoes, white bread, and white rice.

Potential in everyday diet

Breadfruit is used to prepare a wide range of appetizers, dips, beverages, salads, soups, stews, casseroles, main dishes, breads, and desserts (see for example, Ragone et al, 2012). This versatile fruit can be prepared and eaten at all stages of maturity, although it is most often consumed when mature but still firm. At this stage, called "mature," the fruit can be used any way one would use potato, and more. It can be roasted, baked, boiled, or fried, and used in a wide array of recipes. Use it for chips and other snacks, or dry and grind it into gluten-free meal or flour that can used to make bread, pastries, pasta, crackers, biscuits, snack products, and more. It can also be pounded into *pa'i ai* (for poi), similar in texture to taro *pa'i ai*.

Nutrition in breadfruit, potato, white bread and white rice based on 100 g of edible portion.

	Bread-fruit[1]	Potato[2]	White bread[2]	White rice[2]
Protein (g)	4.0	1.7	9.2	2.4
Carbohydrate (g)	31.9	15.7	49.0	29.0
Energy kcal	134.0	69.0	265.0	130.0
Fat (g)	0.2	0.1	3.2	0.2
Fiber (g)	5.4	2.4	2.7	0.3
Calcium (mg)	16.8	9.0	260.0	3.0
Magnesium (mg)	34.3	21.0	25.0	13.0
Phosphorus (mg)	43.1	62.0	103.0	37.0
Potassium (mg)	376.7	407.0	115.0	29.0
Sodium (mg)	19.4	16.0	491.0	0.0
Iron (mg)	0.5	0.5	3.6	0.2
Zinc (mg)	0.1	0.3	0.8	0.4
Vitamin C (mg)	2.4	9.1	0.0	0.0
Thiamin—B$_1$ (mg)	0.1	0.1	0.5	0.0
Riboflavin—B$_2$ (mg)	0.0	0.0	0.2	0.0
Niacin—B$_3$ (mg)	0.9	1.1	4.8	0.4
Vitamin A (µg)	1.4	0.0	0.0	0.0

[1] Breadfruit, raw: average for 'Ulu, Ma'afala, and Meinpadahk. Jones et al. 2011, Ragone & Cavaletto 2006.

[2] White bread (18069), White rice, medium-grain, cooked, unenriched (20451), White potato with skin, raw (11354) from USDA National Nutrient Database for Standard Reference, Release 25, 2012.

BENEFITS OF BEST PRACTICES

Proper handling of breadfruit at all stages will increase shelf life and fruit quality, reduce losses, and help maintain and enhance product value and desirability. Optimal tree health is the basis for high productivity, pest and disease resistance, and large, good quality fruit. Tall trees are difficult and dangerous to harvest, and fruit can easily be damaged by dropping, therefore, annual tree pruning is essential to maintain tree size and shape for ease of harvesting fruit. Harvesting and field handling techniques that minimize blemishes to the fruit also minimize field losses and extend shelf life. Finally, well-planned postharvest handling and storage practices can reduce losses and maximize the amount of fruit that reaches the table.

Good pre-harvest, harvest, and postharvest practices—detailed in this manual—can help producers and retailers deliver excellent quality fruit to chefs

© Craig Elevitch

© Diane Ragone

© Ric Rocker

© Craig Elevitch

Breadfruit can be eaten at all stages of maturity, although mature fruit (bottom left) is best for most dishes. Top left: Small immature fruit can be boiled and has a flavor similar to artichoke hearts—these are delicious pickled or marinated. Top right: Immature fruit is much less flavorful than mature fruit and has a rubbery texture, but can be eaten as a vegetable. Bottom left: Mature fruit has a rich flavor and creamy texture and is preferred for most non-dessert dishes. Bottom right: Soft, ripe fruit is sweet and can be eaten raw or used for desserts, baked goods, and beverages. Note: Immature and mature breadfruit must first be cooked and cannot be eaten raw.

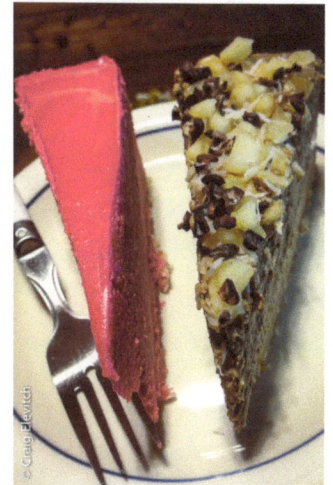

Breadfruit is highly versatile and can be used as an ingredient in hundreds of dishes, potentially giving it a featured place in Hawai'i regional cuisine incorporating Asian and Pacific influences with fresh, locally grown foods. Top: Sam Choy's breadfruit seafood salad and Tahitian roasted breadfruit with fresh coconut cream served with breadfruit chips. Bottom left to right: Sam Choy's breadfruit seafood chowder; 'Āina Ola Culinary Arts Class's 'Ulu & Niu Soufflé; and Pono Pies' panini and chocolate 'ulu pies.

and consumers. Good eating quality is essential for a strong breadfruit market to develop as part of a more food secure Hawai'i. Development of value-added products—based on fruit produced and harvested for specific processes—will help expand markets for the fruit.

PRE-HARVEST

Tree health

Healthy trees grow more vigorously, resist disease, and produce a larger quantity and higher quality of fruit. Fruit trees, as opposed to landscape and horticultural plants, have their own set of requirements due to their biology and fruiting cycle.

A single breadfruit tree can produce hundreds of pounds of fruit each year, consuming significant amounts of nutrients and resources in the process. Breadfruit trees use comparatively more energy and nutritional and mineral resources in fruit production compared to other trees that do not invest significant resources in fruit. Insufficient availability of certain minerals and elements can greatly impact fruit set and size at maturity, as well as tree health and vigor. Therefore, it is important to monitor and ensure that breadfruit trees have sufficient nutrition.

In Hawai'i we are used to seeing large, healthy, productive trees growing in the landscape, seemingly without care. The nutritional needs of trees that are harvested regularly are somewhat higher, as the nutrients taken away with the fruit need to be replaced.

In Hawai'i, we take for granted the large, healthy breadfruit trees that seem to bear fruit year after year without any human intervention. When producing fruit for harvest, the tree's nutritional needs are very important.

The information presented below is directed toward growers who intend on harvesting their breadfruit regularly and will assist anyone in keeping their trees healthy.

Tree health begins from the ground up

Fruit trees, such as breadfruit, expend large amounts of resources and energy producing fruit. Healthy trees require healthy soil, which in turn requires proper orchard sanitation, healthy biology, beneficial cover crops, and the addition of amendments and fertilizers.

Healthy soil biology is achieved by removing fallen fruit and branches (sanitation), closely monitoring fertilizer application, encouraging the growth of beneficial soil microorganisms, and applying high quality mulch and compost. Sanitation by removing fallen fruit and branches can help decrease problems caused by naturally occurring pathogenic microorganisms in the soil (*Fusarium*, *Phytophthora*, *Anthracnose*, *Rhizopus*, etc.), especially in parts of Hawai'i that receive regular rain. Many of the pathogenic spores spread in water during rainstorms. Removing fallen fruit and branches also eliminates additional sources of inoculum.

There are many different techniques and materials for producing mulch and compost. Mulch and compost derived from healthy plant materials can sometimes inhibit the growth of pathogenic microorganisms. High quality mulch is material with a good carbon (C) to nitrogen (N) ratio, which encourages beneficial fungal organisms rather than growth of disease-causing bacteria. Decomposing woody material (with fungal decomposition) can be very beneficial. Mulch is especially important for wet areas or large mature groves with more limited nutrient resources and more shade. Hawai'i soils are often low in available calcium, iron, sulfur, nitrogen and phosphorous, especially in long term agricultural areas. It is recommended that both mulch and compost be applied once or twice a year at a thickness of 16–20 cm (6–8 in) under the tree canopy out to and beyond the drip line.

Fertilizer application can ensure that trees are receiving proper nutrition and can combat any deficiencies or soil conditions that impact nutrient availability. The best place to start, prior to buying fertilizer or designing a fertilizer program, is with soil and/or tissue testing. Soil testing, (a service provided by the University of Hawai'i, Agricultural Diagnostic Service Center), can inform the farmer as to what nutrients are present in the soil, including calcium, and soil pH (Silva and Uchida, Chap. 3). Tissue testing, which is generally done using dried leaves, informs the grower as to which nutrients and elements are present in the plant itself.

A balanced fertilizer program (Silva and Uchida, Chaps. 12, 15) can also add to soil fertility and prevent nutrient deficiencies and excess stress following fruiting or growing seasons. Adding fertilizer annually is generally recommended, preferably before the fruiting season, and immediately after any major pruning events. Growers can successfully use organic or conventional (synthetic) fertilizers. When using conventional fertilizers, a nitrogen-phosphorus-potassium (N-P-K) ratio of about 3-1-2 is recommended. However, testing soil and plant tissue is a more precise method of determining fertilizer needs. As a cautionary note, some believe that the high N-P-K values (16-16-16) found in some synthetic fertilizers can negatively impact beneficial soil microorganisms. Using time-release, and low N-P-K organic fertilizers reduce nutrient leaching, which often takes place in times of high rainfall. Organic fertilizer sources are considered to be more supportive of soil microorganisms as well.

A healthy soil biota is imperative for the proper decomposition of organic material and the capture and release of nutrients for plant uptake. Many growers find it helpful to incorporate soil builders into their fertilization plan, and to use organic treatments such as compost tea, biochar, fermented plant juices, etc. All of these techniques have been used successfully with breadfruit trees and contribute to a healthy and diverse soil biota. Other soil builders available from most garden supply companies in Hawai'i include: greensand, oyster shells, rock phosphate, crushed calcium carbonate (limestone), etc. Each of these has a specific purpose and it is usually best to consult an agricultural professional for recommendations.

Cover crops

Beneficial cover crops can suppress weeds, help build healthy soil structure and biology, provide nutrients and mulch materials, and reduce nutrient leaching. Before establishing cover crops, grass and weed species are removed out to the drip line of the trees. Controlling weeds and grass throughout a farm with cover crops reduces the frequency of mowing and/or brush cutting, saving time and fuel. There are two major types of cover crops that have been used successfully in breadfruit orchards. Permanent ground covers, such as perennial pea-

Cover crops and mulch can suppress weed growth, help retain moisture, add organic material, reduce soil erosion, and help retain available nutrients. Top and center: Permanent cover of the nitrogen fixing vine lablab (*Lablab purpureus*). Bottom: Mulching with composted wood chips.

Throughout the Pacific Islands, breadfruit has traditionally been grown together with other crops in mixed agroforests. These systems have the advantage of providing yields continuously, conserving valuable nutrients, and being more resistant to outbreaks of pests and diseases. This Kona, Hawai'i agroforestry farm includes coconut, banana, ti, coffee, taro, and mountain apple.

nut (*Arachis pintoi* and *A. glabrata*), help suppress grass and weeds. Green manures or soil builders, like comfrey (*Symphytum* spp.) and vetiver (*Chrysopogon zizanioides*), have extensive root systems that shuttle nutrients and minerals from deep in the soil to the surface where they can be incorporated and utilized by trees and soil microorganisms. Nitrogen fixing tree and shrub species, such as gliricidia (*Gliricidia sepium*) and pigeon pea (*Cajanus cajan*), can be regularly cut and laid down or chipped to provide a good source of mulch and steady release of nutrients for the orchard. A combination of multiple species and types of cover crops can reduce the work needed to maintain an orchard while building soil structure, health and fertility.

Agroforestry

Breadfruit has traditionally been grown as one of many crops in complex, multicrop agroforestry systems throughout the Pacific. Breadfruit does well interplanted with a wide array of plants. For example, more than 120 useful species have been documented in traditional breadfruit agroforests on Pohnpei (Raynor and Fownes 1991). Short-term fruit crops (e.g., pineapple, banana, and papaya) or field and vegetable crops (e.g., taro, tomato, and eggplant) can also be grown between young breadfruit trees.

Such diverse systems are thought to have multiple benefits to the crops, the ecosystem, and the grower. For the crops, diverse agroforests can help with plant health by providing important ecological functions such as replenishing the litter layer to protect soil and nutrient cycling. Biodiversity may also reduce

Example breadfruit agroforestry intercrops

Understory	Middle story	Overstory
Various annual vegetables	banana (*Musa* spp.)	betel nut (*Areca catechu*)
pineapple (*Ananas comosus*)	cacao (*Theobroma cacao*)	citrus (*Citrus* spp.)
taro (*Colocasia esculenta*)	coffee (*Coffea arabica*)	coconut (*Cocos nucifera*)
ti (*Cordyline fruticosa*)	kava (*Piper methysticum*)	poumuli (*Flueggea macrophylla*)
yam (*Dioscorea* spp.)	noni (*Morinda citrifolia*)	Tahitian chestnut (*Inocarpus fagifer*)
pumpkin and squash (*Cucurbita* spp.)	papaya (*Carica papaya*)	Various timber trees
	sugarcane (*Saccharum officinarum*)	

Ground covers
Perennial peanut (*Arachis* species)
Lablab (*Lablab purpureus*)

the incidence of certain pests and diseases. For the ecosystem, agroforests can function similar to natural forests in protecting soil and water, fulfilling important watershed functions. For the grower, agroforests provide multiple products, and can increase total yield compared with a single crop.

Pests and diseases

Several plant diseases have been found on breadfruit trees in Hawai'i including *Fusarium*, *Phytophthora*, and fruit *Anthracnose*. However, if trees are healthy, and proper sanitation is maintained by removing fallen fruit, disease problems are usually minimal. Some symptoms that have been observed on unhealthy, unmanaged trees include fruit rot, tip dieback, and root rot. Also, some minor damage to fruit from fruit flies has been observed.

Pruning

It is commonly believed that breadfruit trees do not need to be pruned. Breadfruit trees can be allowed to grow large in certain situations, however, farmers and home growers need to be able to harvest fruit efficiently and safely. Climbing trees to harvest raises safety concerns. It is better to avoid the need for climbing, which can be accomplished by regu-

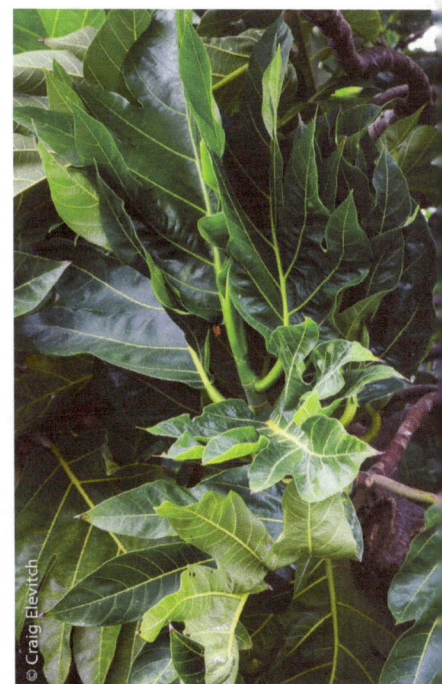

Left: Removing fallen fruit before it rots is an important maintenance activity to help limit spread of fruit diseases. Center: Root suckers are attached to the vascular system of the tree. Therefore, spraying herbicide on root suckers is the same as spraying herbicide on the tree. Unwanted root suckers should be cut off at the base prior to application of herbicide near a breadfruit tree. Right: Curling and bunching of new leaf growth usually indicates herbicide toxicity.

lar pruning to a height of 4.5–5.5 m (15–18 ft). If pruning begins when trees are young and continues annually, trees can be kept at a desired size for decades.

Pruning requires skill and experience. When working with saws and chain saws, it is very easy to make mistakes and damage trees, strip bark, or create unsafe branch unions that fail and break. It is strongly recommended to hire a professional, ISA (International Society of Arboriculture) Certified Arborist. These professionals are trained and are bonded against accidents. At the very least, safe pruning techniques should be learned through a certified training program (local agricultural extension offices can often advise about training opportunities).

In order to keep trees at a manageable height, it is recommended that pruning and shaping begin when trees are young, about 2–3 years old, and continue each year thereafter. This eliminates the need to cut large branches, which results in large wounds

in the tree. Smaller wounds (such as from cutting only small branches) heal much better than large wounds, especially in wet climates.

Pruning larger, mature trees down to a manageable size is possible, however, this is much more difficult. Although the cost is often high, a certified arborist can give expert advice, use trained personnel with proper technique and equipment, and is licensed, insured and bonded. Larger branches sometimes need to be removed. This can cause damage by

© Craig Elevitch

Breadfruit trees should be shaped by pruning yearly to stimulate new growth and keep the fruit within easy harvesting height. Pruning to a height of 4.5–5.5 m (15–18 ft) greatly increases harvesting efficiency.

Pruning young trees

For young trees, it is important to control vigorous shoots both from the top and sides. Crown reduction throughout the canopy—rather than only topping—is the best practice.

The first pruning should be done as needed, usually by Year 3 or 4. Prune back to a strong branch union. Take care to remove aggressive shoots and co-dominant leaders. Prune only branches that need to be pruned to shape the tree to an even domed canopy.

A pruning height of 4.5–5.5 m (15–18 ft) is recommended. Prune back to the same height each year. Consult a professional arborist for guidance.

Top: A professional arborist should be hired for reducing the size of large trees. Bottom: In many Pacific Islands, such as here in Upolu, Samoa, annual pruning is an age-old practice to prevent breadfruit trees to facilitate harvesting and for safety reasons during high wind events.

stripping large sections of bark from the trunk, or by falling on and breaking lower branches as they come down. Professional arborists often need to rig larger sections and lower them with winches and ropes to eliminate damage. All of these techniques require special training and specialized equipment to prevent unnecessary damage to trees and injury to the arborist.

Pruning should ideally take place after a tree has finished fruiting and before the growth stage has really kicked in. These pruning events should be followed by application of fertilizer, mulch, and compost, thereby making essential nutrients and minerals available to the tree. Some orchard managers in Hawai'i fertilize, mow cover crops, and apply fresh mulch immediately after pruning. It is important to remember that pruning is stressful to trees and results in open wounds that need to heal. Any extra care you can give your trees—such as maintaining optimal soil moisture and fertility—following pruning will help them get through the associated stress.

HARVEST

Even though breadfruit is edible at any stage of development, it is essential to understand and recognize the different stages of fruit development and maturity, and harvest fruit at the optimal stage for the desired market or use. Fruit that are picked too green and still immature have a longer shelf life than fruit harvested at the full mature stage, which explains why immature fruit is often sold in supermarkets and at farmers markets. However, immature fruit is undesirable for most dishes. Such fruit has a rubbery texture and characterless flavor unsuitable for most dishes where a creamy texture and rich flavor are desired. Immature fruit will become soft over time, but does not ripen, making it unacceptable for dishes requiring ripe fruit. For many chefs and consumers, immature breadfruit is their first introduction to this food, and the negative experience often discourages them buying or eating it again.

On the other hand, most people who try a dish prepared with firm, mature fruit enjoy it immediately.

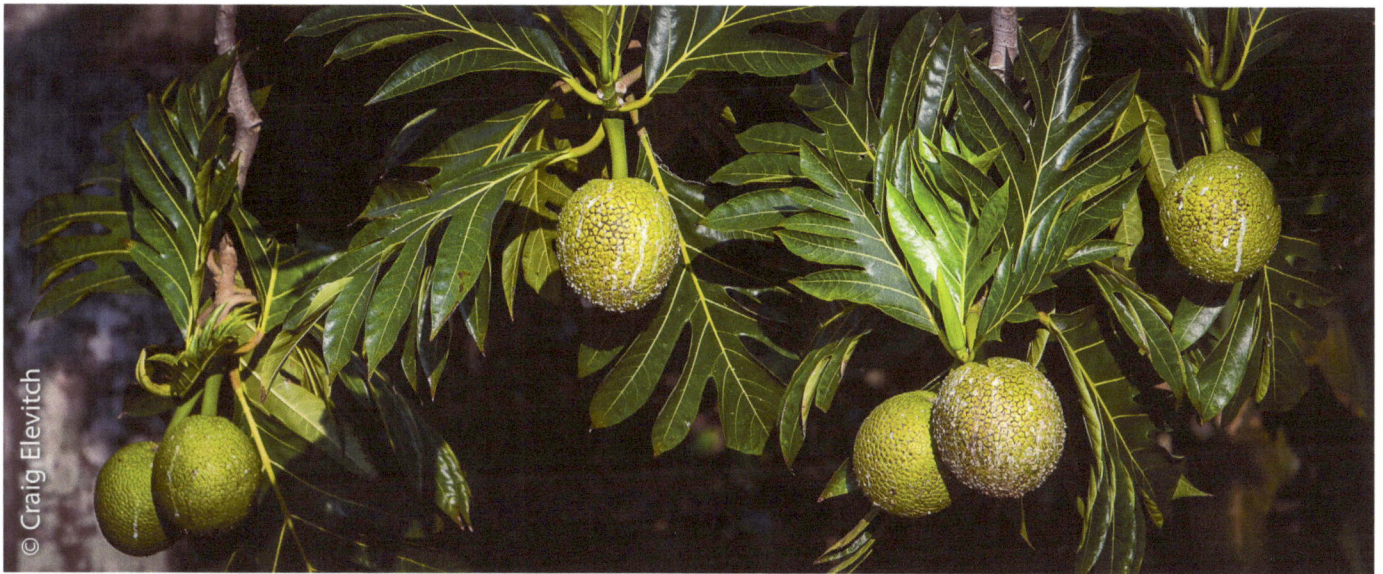
© Craig Elevitch

For most end uses, mature fruit is needed. Flowering takes place over several weeks, meaning that the fruits on any given tree are at a range of development stages, therefore

Therefore, most experienced breadfruit consumers demand mature fruit. High quality mature fruit has the highest value in the marketplace. Challenges to providing mature fruit include harvesting each fruit at the right maturity stage over a period of several weeks, minimizing damage during transport and storage, and storage. Fruit should be held in the best storage conditions to maximize postharvest life. Addressing these challenges will ensure high palatability of the end product and help increase consumer acceptance and demand.

It is important to understand the process of development from young inflorescence (hundreds of individual flowers on a central core that fuse together) into mature fruit. Fruit generally reach full mature size and develop maximum starch levels (creamy texture and full flavor) at 16–20± weeks from the time the tiny fruit emerges from the end of the branch, giving the producer a 5-week period over which mature fruit can be harvested. Harvesting at the beginning stages of maturity is the best option for fruit that will be shipped interisland, will be stored for a few days before use, or will be fried into chips. At the intermediate stages of maturity, the fruit has the greatest range of uses. Fruit that ripens on the tree is often damaged during harvest. Because fully mature fruit will ripen after harvest, the

trees must be harvested at least once per week to optimize high quality yields. Based on the variety, environment and weather, some trees can bear almost continuously.

most mature fruit are ideal for the chef or consumer who will use soft and sweet ripened fruit.

In this guide, the terminology used for the different marketable categories of maturity is:

Immature: A young fruit at any stage of development before reaching full size.

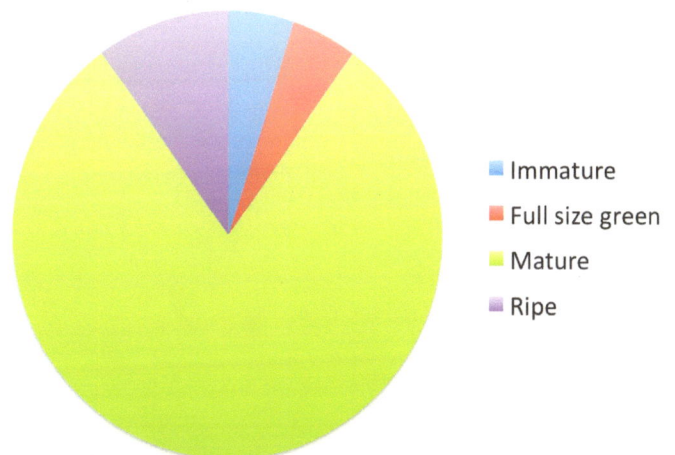

Legend:
- Immature
- Full size green
- Mature
- Ripe

Authors' estimate of the relative market sizes for different maturity stages:

Immature 5% (taste like artichokes); full size green 5% (for chips and other dishes that require a vegetable-like, firm flesh); mature 80% (for dishes that require a potato-like starch including salad, fries, curry, soups, stew, etc., as well as many processed products); and, ripe 10% (for desserts such as sweet baked goods, pies, ice cream, etc.).

| Flowering | Immature | Full size green | Mature | Ripe |

| 0 weeks | | | ≈16 weeks | | ≈20 weeks | |

Immature fruit consumed as vegetable. Not preferred for most dishes.

Mature fruit consumed as starch. Preferred for most dishes.

Ripe fruit consumed in sweet dishes

Breadfruit can be eaten at all stages of development. However, mature fruit (about 16–20 weeks of development after flowering) has the best eating qualities for most uses.

Generic fruit development table

	Development stage	Description/uses	Photo
	Flowering (0 weeks)	Breadfruit has both female and male inflorescences. The female inflorescences, which we commonly called fruit, are edible at any stage of development. Very young fruit have similar taste and texture to artichoke.	
	Immature (0–16 weeks)	The deep green fruit at an immature stage of development has a firm, rubbery texture and can be used as a vegetable in dishes.	
	Full size green (about 12–16 weeks*)	This is an immature fruit that has reached full size. Despite its longer shelf life, it is not preferred by most consumers. It can be used as a vegetable, but it has not developed starchy characteristics.	

Generic fruit development table (con't)

Development stage	Description/uses	Photo
Mature (16–18 weeks*)	Mature fruit has developed into a starchy staple with smooth texture and good flavor. It is preferred for most dishes including stews, soups, curries, fries, etc. Fruit harvested in the first two weeks of the mature phase has a longer shelf life than fruit harvested during the second two weeks of maturity.	
Mature (18–20 weeks*)	Fruit harvested in the latter stages of maturity has excellent eating qualities, but a shorter shelf life than fruit harvested earlier.	
Half-ripe	After maturity the fruit eventually turns from a starchy staple into a ripe dessert fruit. Half-ripe fruit has begun converting starches into sugars and has a similar texture and sweetness to sweetpotato—still slightly firm and moderately sweet. It can be eaten cooked like sweet potato and used in a variety of dishes.	
Ripe	The fruit eventually turns into a ripe dessert fruit. At this stage the fruit is very soft and emits a sweet, fruity fragrance. Ripe fruit can be used raw (similar to a custard) or cooked in many types of desserts including cakes, cookies, pies, etc.	

* This range is based on a single study of fruit of a typical triploid Polynesian variety similar to the Hawaiian 'Ulu. Data have yet to be collected for Ma'afala, 'Ulu, Micronesian hybrid, and other varieties. Therefore, this time range should be considered a general guide only.

Delivering breadfruit harvested at the correct stage of maturity is essential for increasing consumer preference.

Full size green: An immature fruit that has reached full size.

Mature: A full size, firm fruit that has become starchy.

Ripe: A mature fruit that has become soft and the starches have been converted to sugars.

Good communication between growers and consumers is essential to delivering quality fruit in the best condition at the desired stages of development: immature and green, mature and starchy, or ready to ripen. Commercial growers should provide chefs and consumers with a selection of fruit at varying stages of maturity so they can become familiar with their attributes and experiment with ways to prepare them. Satisfied and knowledgeable consumers will increase their consumption of fresh breadfruit.

FRUIT MATURITY INDICATORS

Every variety of breadfruit has its own indicators for fruit maturity. Although the following maturity indicators are not universal for all varieties, they ap-

Maturity indicators for 'Ulu (Hawaiian) and Ma'afala varieties

Skin color turns from bright green to green-yellow and Skin texture changes from pointy or bumpy to smooth and flat	 Immature Ma'afala	 Mature Ma'afala
Natural cracks in the skin begin dripping sap	 Immature 'Ulu	 Mature 'Ulu

Maturity indicators for 'ulu (Hawaiian) and Ma'afala varieties

Fissures in the skin form as the fruit matures, forming dark, crusty lines	 Immature 'Ulu	 Mature 'Ulu
Stem color changes from deep green to lighter green or yellow-green	 Immature 'Ulu	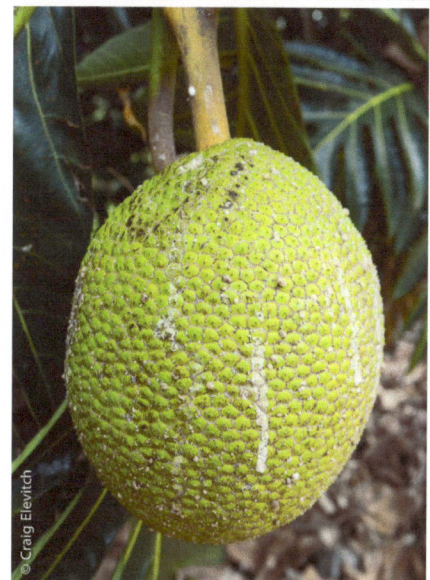 Mature 'Ulu
Flesh immediately under the skin turns from green to white or cream color, sap is reduced in mature fruit	 Immature Ma'afala	 Mature Ma'afala

Maturity indicators for Meinpadahk (Micronesian variety)

Skin turns from bright green to yellow-green to pale yellow with green lines between sections turning yellow to yellow-brown. The sections may also slightly separate. There is typically no scabbing on sections and little sap on the skin.

Immature Meinpadahk

Mature Mainpadahk

Left: immature, Right: mature

Mature Meinpadahk

Flesh immediately under the skin turns from green to pale yellow, sap is reduced in mature fruit

Immature Meinpadahk

Mature Meinpadahk

ply to many varieties present in Hawai'i. Not all indicators are always present in mature fruit. Some indicators can be deceptive. For example, sap drip may be caused by wind damage to an immature fruit. Therefore several indicators should be present to have reasonable certainty about fruit maturity.

Draining sap

Every part of the breadfruit tree, including the fruit, contains a white, sticky sap (also called latex). In the fruit the sap is concentrated in the skin and around the core. This sticky sap can adhere to kitchenware during the cutting and cooking process, and is often the cause of complaints by people who are new to breadfruit. Harvesting fully mature fruit and allowing the sap to drain from the fruit immediately after harvest can greatly reduce or eliminate the presence

of sap in the kitchen. A recommended method for draining the sap is to cut the stem close to the base and then setting the fruit on the stem end on a clean surface for about an hour. Resting the fruit on the cut stem reduces the amount of sap that adheres on the fruit surface during the draining process.

Left: Sap oozes from the cut end of the stem. Care should be taken to drain the sap onto a clean surface so that it does not adhere to the skin and complicated clean-up. Right: Cutting the stem close to the skin—without cutting into the fruit skin itself—and resting the fruit on cut stem allows the sap to drain freely and minimizes clean-up.

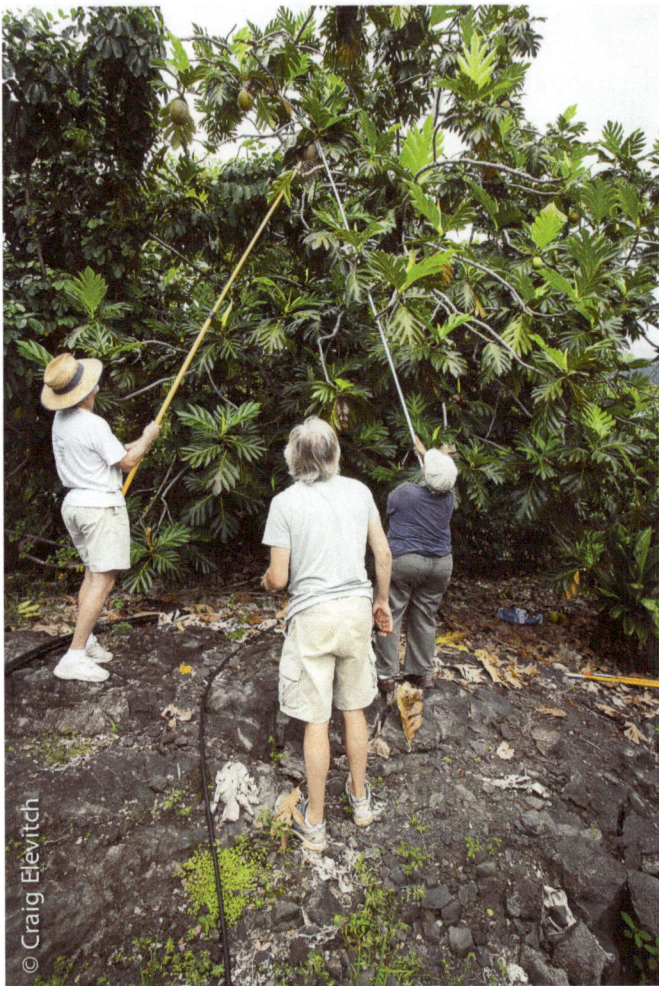

How many people does it take to harvest a breadfruit without letting it fall to the ground? Answer: Just one, provided the proper tools are used.

General harvesting concerns

A goal of harvesting is to remove fruit with minimal damage to the fruit or the tree. This goal becomes increasingly more difficult to achieve with tall trees. Harvesting from tall trees presents added dangers from falling fruit, unsteady equipment, etc. Therefore, controlling tree size through regular pruning (see "Pruning" section) is an essential component of an efficient and effective harvesting program.

Fruit that is allowed to fall to the ground will be bruised externally and internally, and has a shorter postharvest life and is more subject to disease. For home use, it can be consumed within a day or two. However, because of the reduction in fruit quality and requirement of food safety best practices that fruit never touch the ground, fallen fruit should not be used commercially.

Harvesting safety

Although tempting to many, climbing breadfruit trees for harvesting is not recommended due to the inherent dangers of loose footing, breaking branches, falling fruit, etc. Climbing should only be attempted in healthy trees by those with certified safety training and equipment (harness, ropes, etc.).

Climbing becomes unnecessary for trees that are regularly pruned to a height of 4.5–5.5 m (15–18 ft). When harvesting from taller trees, a sturdy platform (such as a truck bed or agricultural lift) or an orchard ladder can be used to extend reach.

Hard hat and eye protection are essential gear for harvesters. Fruit, dead branches, and other debris can inadvertently fall, presenting danger of injury to those below. Head and eye protection are simple and convenient precautions well worth taking.

Some harvesters attempt to have one person cut the fruit stem while another person stands underneath the tree to catch the fruit. Due to the unpredictable way fruit can bounce off of branches as they fall, attempting to catch fruit is too dangerous in most situations as well as resulting in many hitting the ground.

A significant portion of fruit on properly pruned trees can efficiently and safely be harvested from the ground by breaking off the stem by hand, without requiring tools.

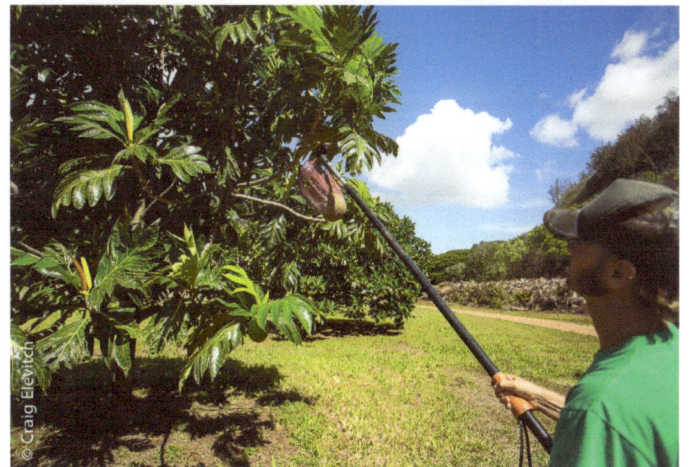

Top: Pole-mounted basket can be twisted to break off fruit stem after placing the stem into a narrow bend in the strong wire rim. Middle: Telescoping cut 'n hold pruner can easily harvest and hold fruit up to 2 kg (4.5 lb). Bottom left: Traditional picker of Micronesia. Bottom right: Telescoping bypass pruner fitted with small basket to catch fruit.

Picking tools

The most efficient and safest way to harvest breadfruit is to use a 3–5 m (10–16 ft) long picking tool while standing on the ground or on a sturdy platform. The best picking tools cut or break the fruit stem and then hold or catch the fruit. A combination of cutting tool (clippers, knife blade, etc.) and net basket is a favorite design of many harvesters.

Keeping cool in the field

Freshly harvested breadfruit has been warmed by the sun and air (field heat) and continues to generate heat from internal respiration. This heat accelerates the ripening process. Setting harvested fruit in the sun can quickly cause sunburn, greatly decreasing market value or destroying the fruit. Therefore, during the harvesting process, fruit should be kept in the shade as much as possible to avoid adding to the field heat. Harvesting fruit in the very early morning hours and late afternoon also helps reduce field heat of harvested fruit.

Fruit should be cooled rapidly in postharvest processing (see "Postharvest" below).

Carrying container during harvest

Containers for carrying and transporting harvested fruit should be sturdy and well ventilated, and allow for one or two layers of fruit at most. More than two layers of fruit can lead to bruising and degradation

A recommended carrying container for harvest allows for good ventilation.

of fruit quality, as well as increased heat build-up. Plastic crates are a good choice for field harvesting and brief storage periods. Cardboard produce boxes with good ventilation can also be used. Large bags such as coffee and onion bags should be avoided, as they restrict airflow and cause bruising and abrasion as they shift in transport. Deep plastic tubs without side ventilation should not be used for similar reasons.

POSTHARVEST

Importance of postharvest practices

Once breadfruit has been harvested, it is important to handle it carefully so that it arrives at its intended destination with minimal quality degradation. Breadfruit is susceptible to bruising (causing discoloration of the skin and flesh, as well as release of sap), ripening, and decay when handled improperly. Postharvest refers to all practices involved in preparing or storing the fruit for sale, cooking, and processing. Good postharvest practices maintain or increase crop quality, safeguard food safety, and minimize losses. More importantly, high quality, unblemished fruit will fetch the best prices. Conversely, poor postharvest practices reduce the quality of the fruit for its intended use, leading to lower prices from customers and higher losses. An example that many breadfruit farmers have experienced is ripening caused by storing breadfruit in suboptimal conditions, ruining the fruit for the firm-mature market. Good postharvest practices are essential for reliably delivering fruit in the condition that customers want, especially high-end markets such as chefs and retailers.

These are the postharvest areas that are important for breadfruit:

- Handling—should minimize bruising or other injury, maintain temperature and air circulation.
- Cleaning—includes washing, brushing, air blowing, etc.
- Sorting—often done just after harvesting to sort out blemished or rotting fruits and group by variety, size, maturity, and quality grade.

- Packing and packaging materials—protect fruit from damage and allow for some air circulation.
- Decay and insect control—carried out through environmental control, cold or heat treatments, oxygen exclusion, pest control, and other methods.
- Temperature, relative humidity, and light control—maintains quality in storage by reducing respiration and rate of water loss.
- Food safety practices—elimination of post-harvest problems that arise from physical and chemical hazards and human pathogens.

Preventing skin damage, discoloration

For certain markets, such as direct to consumers or retail sales, unblemished fruit commands the highest price. Damage can occur in several stages: on the tree during high winds, during harvest (addressed in the previous section), and after harvest in cleaning, sorting, packaging, storage, and transportation.

Slowing ripening

Mature breadfruit will ripen at room temperature in 1–3 days, depending on the temperature, relative humidity, ventilation, and variety. Slowing the process of ripening is essential for the fresh fruit market, as customers for mature breadfruit are usually not interested in ripe fruit (although there are other markets for ripe fruit that should be considered once fruit has ripened).

Food safety (after Elevitch and Love, 2013)

Food safety certification is increasingly becoming important to customers, especially for larger retailers, distributors, restaurants, etc. Many distributors require food safety certification and liability insurance and these requirements are expected to become universal. Because certification can require high expenditures for infrastructure, small farm enterprises may not initially be able to justify the cost. However, all farm operations should closely follow Good Agricultural Practices (GAPs), a set of guidelines that are the basis for food safety certification. In Hawai'i, laws such as where certain processed foods can be prepared and sold, and local building permitting

policies vary from island to island and sometimes between regions on an island.

A few of the practices required that relate to harvesting breadfruit include (excerpted from CTAHR undated):

- Using a proactive pest management strategy for rodents, birds, deer, pigs, slugs and snails.
- Keeping animals and their fresh manures away from active fields and orchards.
- Following the U.S. EPA Worker Protection Standard rules.
- Making sure that produce and harvest baskets with holes in them do not come in contact with the soil or unclean surfaces.
- Using appropriate quality water for irrigation and crop rinse, as indicated by a water test from an approved laboratory.
- Making sure the packing shed, food contact packing surfaces, and refrigerators are well maintained and not a potential source of contamination.

For breadfruit producers, this means in practice:

- Fruit should not be allowed to come into contact with soil or contaminated surfaces, including when draining sap after harvest.
- Harvesting containers should be kept clean.
- Rodent or bird infestations should be addressed.
- Fruit should be gently rinsed in clean water in an approved facility to remove loose debris before shipping.

For more information on food safety certification, see "CTAHR Good Agricultural Practices Coaching" (CTAHR undated).

Contact your local Hawai'i State Department of Health office for specific information about food handling facilities and the Pacific Agrosecurity & Food Safety Program of the University of Hawai'i (www.manoa.hawaii.edu/ctahr/pacific-afsp/?pageid=127) for more information about food safety certification.

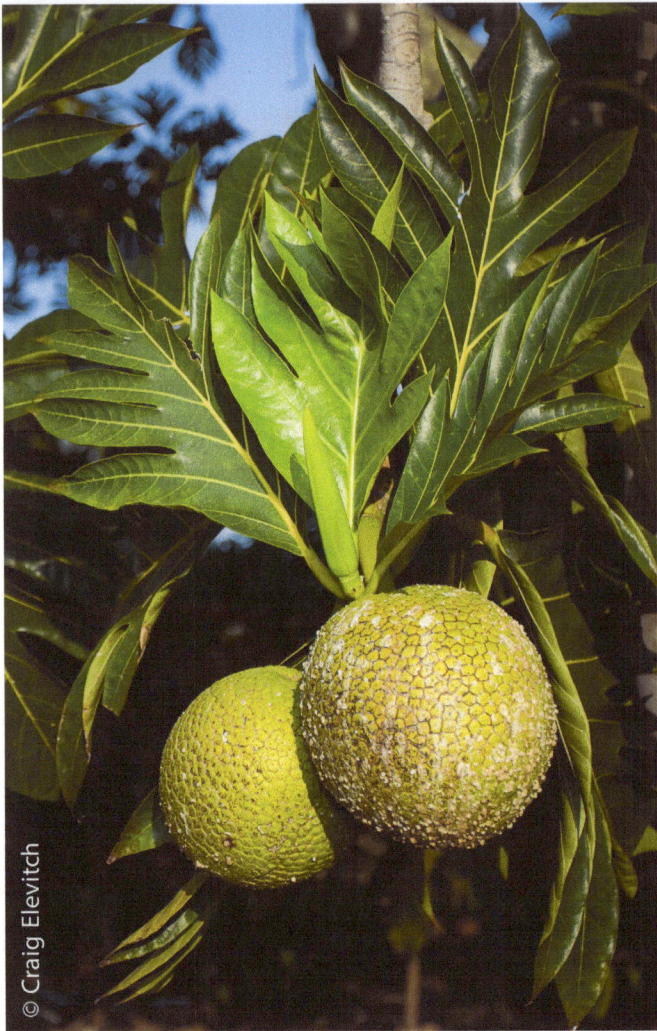

Quality characteristics of an ideal breadfruit include correct maturity stage, lack of blemishes, sap drained, transported without damage, and storage in proper conditions to optimize shelf life and appearance.

Preparing for packaging, storage, and consumption

Proper harvest techniques are essential for delivering a quality product. As covered in the previous section, picking at the proper stage of maturity, preventing fruit from dropping on the ground, observing food safety practices, and draining fruit sap immediately after harvest all contribute to favorable product quality. Damaged fruit should be packed in separate containers immediately after harvest, as well as being washed and cooled in separate water to minimise cross contamination.

Cooling

Fruit is warmed by the sun and air. After harvest, a breadfruit generates its own heat from continu-

ing respiration. Often the warmth of the fruit can be felt hours after harvest, unless measures are taken to cool the fruit. The combination of environmental and internally generated warmth, or "field heat," hastens the ripening process, so fruit should be cooled as soon as possible after harvest. At a minimum, harvested fruit should immediately be allowed to drain sap and then kept in well ventilated open boxes placed in the shade (not in direct sunlight). Alternatively, fruit can be harvested in the early morning before they have been warmed by the sun and at all times kept in the shade to drain covered by shade cloth or cardboard. Depending on transport time to the washing and packing facility, other options for field cooling include immersing the fruit in cool water (see "Washing/cleaning" below), refrigeration (see "Refrigeration" below), or covering the fruit with a layer of crushed ice.

A cold water or ice bath for 10–15 minutes removes field heat and can greatly prolong shelf life. Soaking for too long can cause brown discoloration of the skin.

For holding small quantities of fruit for a day or so, rinse the fruit, put in a cooler, and cover with crushed ice or ice cubes. Replenish the ice as it melts or submerge fruit in cold water. For shipping, drain out the water and wrap each fruit in newspaper to cushion it and help insulate. The spaces between fruits can be stuffed with newspaper as well to help cushion. A frozen blue ice block wrapped in newspaper in a plastic bag can also be included to help keep the contents cool.

Ice option

For short-term storage and to remove field heat, breadfruit can be placed into tubs containing icy water for 10–15 minutes. The fruit quickly cools as the ice melts. Prolonged storage in icy water may cause brown discoloration of the skin due to chilling injury.

Washing/cleaning

A gentle rinsing with water, air blowing, or gently brushing with a soft bristle brush can be employed to remove loose debris from the surface of the fruit, particularly around the stem where organic debris and insects tend to accumulate. Pressure washing or vigorous brushing should be avoided, as these methods abrade the skin leading to additional release of sap and opening potential entry points for decay organisms.

A water bath immediately after harvest is often used commercially to lift off debris, insects, and some of the hardened sap naturally exuded onto the fruit surface. Rapid removal of field heat is an added advantage of a water bath. There should be plenty of room in the bath for fruits to float freely, rather than pressing against each other, causing abrasion. Bath water should be changed frequently to remove accumulated sap and foreign material.

Sorting by size, maturity, quality, variety

After washing/cleaning it is important to sort fruit for various uses and markets. Many customers, such as retailers, whose clientele is accustomed to perfect, uniform fruit, and restaurants, who make a uniform product, such as breadfruit chips, prefer first grade fruit and will pay more for it. Certain customers, such as chefs who include chunks of breadfruit in various dishes, accept smaller or irregular fruit as a cost savings. Because individual breadfruit varieties may require somewhat different cooking or processing, different varieties should be sold separately and clearly marked with the variety name.

Off-grade fruit include those that have a misshapen form, mechanical damage from harvesting, internal or external bruising, various surface lesions, or other imperfection that compromises quality. In addition to removing fruit that are off-grade (usually unacceptable for selling for human consumption), sorting prepares fruit to sell at the highest value for various markets.

Grading

Fruit grading is used for sales of bulk quantities. There are currently no nationally or internationally accepted grading standards for breadfruit, with the desired size and weight varying by variety and market. Suggested general grading standards for green mature fruit include (after Paull and Chen 2004):

First grade	Desired size and weight (varies by variety), mature, fully formed, uniform shape, free from decay, sunscald, cracks, bruises, and mechanical damage.
Second grade	Less than desired size and weight, mature, fully formed, slight blemishes, free from decay, sunscald, cracks, bruises, and mechanical damage.
Off-grade (for processing or animal feed)	Misshapen, bruised, fissured, split, rodent/bird damaged, sunburned, soft spots, decay, stem torn below base, etc.

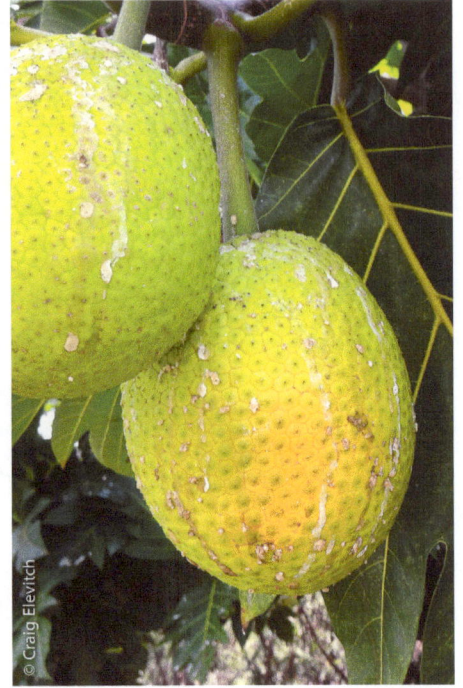

Fruit should be sorted after harvesting to remove off-grade material. Left: Disease legion on fruit. Middle: A very mature, but still firm fruit has surface cracking. Such fruit is excellent for home use, but not for commercial sale. Right: Sunscald on fruits leads to uneven maturation and often to disease legions forming on the surface.

No current size standards exist for Hawaiian breadfruit. A hypothetical example of standards for mature fruit of the variety Maʻafala in Hawaiʻi is:

Size	Diameter (narrow dimension)	Weight
Large	>13 cm (5 in)	>900 g (2 lb)
Medium	10–13 cm (4–5 in)	700–900 g (1.5–2 lb)
Small	8–10 cm (3–4 in)	450–700 g (1 lb–1.5 lb)
Off grade	<8 cm (<3 in)	<450 g (<1 lb)

Storage

Ideally fruit is harvested, sorted, cleaned, packaged and delivered shortly thereafter to the customer for immediate use. This can be impractical for many reasons, so proper storage conditions are important to maintain quality.

Room temperature

Room temperature storage is the least preferred method, as green mature fruit will usually ripen and soften within one to three days. Good ventilation can help reduce the rate of ripening.

Submerged in water

As a low tech, readily available storage option, keeping breadfruit fully submerged in cool, clean fresh water can maintain quality for a week or longer. Keeping the water temperature at about 13°C (55°F) removes field heat and slows internal respiration. Warm water tends to cause swelling and splitting of the fruit, and therefore should be avoided. Any part of the fruit that is above water will ripen and/or soften rapidly. Because breadfruit floats in water, a weight of some type should be used to hold the fruit completely under water. The container and weight should be made from food safety certified materials and be kept clean using food-safe cleaners. The water should be changed daily. Fruit that is in an advanced state of maturity may take on water through fissures in the skin and develop severe cracks. Growers are advised to exercise caution using this method. As described in NWC (2005), "Research by Worrell and Carrington (1997) in Barbados found that fruit submerged and held at 13°C (55°F), with daily changes of water, retained a bright green colour for almost 3 weeks (p. 352)."

Refrigeration (after Paull and Chen 2004)

Storage in a standard household refrigerator leads to skin browning, which is not acceptable for most commercial markets, although fruit quality is not degraded significantly. Optimal refrigeration is carried out at 12–14°C (54–57°F) and 90–95% RH (relative humidity), which can maintain fruit quality for a maximum of about 20 days. On a retail produce shelf, the temperature should be 12–14°C (54–57°F) with no misting. Below 12°C (54°F), chilling injuries include browning of the skin, failure to ripen normally, poor flavor development, and an increase in decay.

Packaging

Fruit is usually sold by weight. A ventilated produce carton that holds 9–18 kg (20–40 lb) is suitable. Cartons should be strong enough to support the weight of stacking cartons on top of them—3–4 cartons high is standard. Some shippers recommend waxed cartons with full-length dividers for export purposes (NWC 2005). Waxed cardboard minimizes softening from water absorption and the dividers keep individual fruit from abrading against each other during transport. Cardboard dividers should also be used between vertically stacked layers of fruit in each box. Plastic crates are also used for transport and short term (1–2 day) storage. At

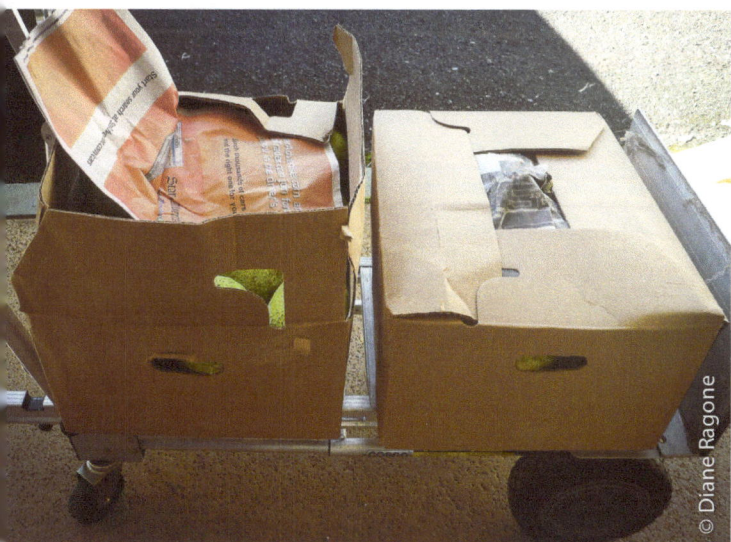

Packaging for shipping should allow adequate ventilation, only one or two layers of fruit, and be strong enough to support stacking 3–4 cartons high without crushing.

all times cartons and crates should not be overfilled to avoid damaging the fruit.

Quarantine treatment

According to Paull and Chen (2004), breadfruit can successfully be treated for fruit fly using vapor heat treatment or irradiation. Export of fresh breadfruit from Hawai'i to the U.S. mainland is allowable after approved irradiation and fungicide treatments. See USDA APHIS-PPQ (2011) for further details.

REFERENCES AND RECOMMENDED READING

Publications

CTAHR. Undated. CTAHR Good Agricultural Practices Coaching. www.manoa.hawaii.edu/ctahr/farmfoodsafety/ [accessed September 26, 2013]

Department of Commerce. 2010. The Native Hawaiian and Other Pacific Islander Population: 2010. 2010 Census Briefs. http://www.census.gov/prod/cen2010/briefs/c2010br-12.pdf

Elevitch, C., and K. Love. 2013. Adding Value to Locally Grown Crops in Hawai'i: A Guide for Small Farm Enterprise Innovation. Permanent Agriculture Resources, Holualoa, Hawai'i. www.valueadded.info

Hawaii Foodbank. 2012. Hawaii Foodbank Annual Report 2011–2012. www.hawaiifoodbank.org

Jones, A.M.P., D. Ragone, K. Aiona, W.A. Lane, and S.J. Murch. 2011. Nutritional and morphological diversity of breadfruit (*Artocarpus,* Moraceae): identification of elite cultivars for food security. *Journal of Food Composition and Analysis* 24 (8):1091–1102.

Lincoln, N.K., N. Wilhoite, K. Friday, J. Eastling, J. Stell-Fresquez, J. Nahakuelua. 2012. An Analysis of Habitat and Distribution of Hawaiian 'Ulu. Unpublished report.

McGregor, A.M. 2002. Growing and Marketing Breadfruit as a Commercial Crop. Fruit Tree Development Project. Ministry of Agriculture, Forests and Meteorology. Samoa.

Macartney, S., A. Bishaw, and K. Fonteno. 2013. Poverty Rates for Selected Detailed Race and Hispanic Groups by State and Place: 2007–2011. American

Community Survey Briefs. http://www.census.gov/prod/2013pubs/acsbr11-17.pdf

Natures Way Cooperative (NWC). 2005. A Manual for the Growing and Marketing of Breadfruit for Export. Natures Way Cooperative, Ltd., Fiji.

Paull, R.E., and N.J. Chen. 2004. Breadfruit. In: K.C. Gross, C.Y. Wang, M. Saltveit. The Commercial Storage of Fruits, Vegetables, and Florist and Nursery Stocks. Agricultural Handbook Number 66.

Ragone, D. 2006. *Artocarpus altilis* (Breadfruit). In: Elevitch, C.R. (ed.). Traditional Trees of Pacific Islands: Their culture, environment, and use. Permanent Agriculture Resources (PAR), Hōlualoa, Hawai'i. http://www.traditionaltree.org

Ragone, D. 2006. *Artocarpus mariannensis* (Dugdug). In: Elevitch, C.R. (ed.). Traditional Trees of Pacific Islands: Their culture, environment, and use. Permanent Agriculture Resources (PAR), Hōlualoa, Hawai'i. http://www.traditionaltree.org

Ragone, D., and C.G. Cavaletto. 2006. Sensory evaluation of fruit quality and nutritional composition of 20 breadfruit (*Artocarpus*, Moraceae) cultivars. *Economic Botany* 60(4):335–346.

Ragone, D. 2011. Farm and Forestry Production and Marketing Profile for Breadfruit (*Artocarpus altilis*). In: Elevitch, C.R. (ed.). Specialty Crops for Pacific Island Agroforestry. Permanent Agriculture Resources (PAR), Hōlualoa, Hawai'i. http://agroforestry.net/scps

Ragone, D., C. Elevitch, D. Shapiro, A. Dean. 2012. Ho'oulu ka 'Ulu Cookbook: Breadfruit tips, techniques, and Hawai'i's favorite home recipes. Breadfruit Institute of the National Tropical Botanical Garden, Kalaheo, Hawai'i and Hawai'i Homegrown Food Network, Holualoa, Hawai'i. www.breadfruit.org and www.breadfruit.info

Raynor, W.C., and J.H. Fownes. 1991. Indigenous agroforestry of Pohnpei 1. Plant species and cultivars. Agroforestry Systems 16: 139–157.

Silva, J.A., and R. Uchida (eds.) 2000. Plant Nutrient Management in Hawaii's Soils, Approaches for Tropical and Subtropical Agriculture, College of Tropical Agriculture and Human Resources, University of Hawaii at Manoa. http://www.ctahr.hawaii.edu/ctahr2001/PIO/FreePubs/PlantNutrient.asp

U.S. Census Bureau. U.S. Department of Commerce. State and County Quick Facts. Hawaii. http://quickfacts.census.gov/qfd/states/15000.html

USDA APHIS-PPQ. 2011. Regulation and Clearance from Hawaii to Other Parts of the United States. USDA, Washington, DC. http://www.aphis.usda.gov/import_export/plants/manuals/ports/downloads/hawaii.pdf

USDA Agricultural Research Service. 2012. USDA National Nutrient Database for Standard Reference, Release 25. Nutrient Data Laboratory Home Page, http://www.ars.usda.gov/ba/bhnrc/ndl

Worrell, D.B., and C.M. Carrington. 1997. Breadfruit. Postharvest Physiology and Storage of Tropical and Subtropical Crops. S.K. Mitra (ed). CAB International.

Web sites

Breadfruit varieties, education, news, recipes, etc.: http://www.breadfruit.org

Breadfruit education: http://www.breadfruit.info

Breadfruit in healthy Pacific diet: https://www.spc.int/hpl/index.php?option=com_content&task=blogcategory&id=17&Itemid=46

Compost Tea: http://www.westernsare.org/Learning-Center/Project-Products/Tea-Time-in-the-Tropics

Cover Crops and Green Manures for Hawai'i: http://www.ctahr.hawaii.edu/sustainag/cc-gm/index.html

Food safety extension publications at UH: http://www.ctahr.hawaii.edu/hnfas/publications.html

Department of Health Food Safety: http://health.hawaii.gov/san/food-information/

APPENDIX 1: BRIEF BREADFRUIT BASICS

PICK IT RIGHT!

Mature fruit has the best flavor and texture for most dishes where a potato-like consistency is desired. It's perfect for eating plain or with a sauce, or for making breadfruit salad, stew, curry, fries and many more kinds of dishes.

Note: A firm, mature breadfruit will ripen and become soft in 1–3 days at room temperature (it can then be used for dessert dishes!). To store a mature fruit and delay ripening, put it in the refrigerator. The skin will turn brown, but the edible flesh will stay firm. Fruit can also be stored a few days fully submerged in cool water (put a weight on top so the fruit is completely underneath the water).

Mature fruit: Look for greenish-yellow skin, a smooth surface, and brownish cracking between the surface segments. The flesh inside is firm and creamy white or pale yellow in color. Some varieties vary in maturity indicators.

RIPE BREADFRUIT IS GREAT FOR DESSERTS

A ripe breadfruit is soft to the touch with a sweet, aromatic fragrance. Ripe fruit is perfect for cakes, pies, cookies, energy bars and other sweet treats.

Ripe breadfruit is best used right away, although it can be kept in the refrigerator for a few days before using or stored in the freezer for later use.

IMMATURE "GREEN" BREADFRUIT SHOULD BE AVOIDED!

Immature breadfruit is bright green and has not reached full size.

Immature fruit is rubbery and watery even when cooked, lacking the rich flavor and texture of mature fruit. An immature breadfruit will not mature or ripen after picking. Most people who eat immature breadfruit end up not liking breadfruit. This is a shame … choose mature breadfruit!

Avoid immature green fruit. An immature, full size fruit is bright green and bumpy and the lines between sections are solid green. The flesh is pale green just beneath the skin. When cooked, the texture is rubbery and the flavor is watery.

DON'T BE SAPPY

Breadfruit contains a small amount of white sap, which can stick to knives, pots and steamers. Cutting off the stem immediately after harvest and letting the fruit sit stem end down drains most of the sap. Sap issues can be reduced or eliminated by choosing mature fruit, proper field handling, washing and refrigeration. In the kitchen, breadfruit should be soaked for 1–2 minutes in cold, clean water and washed to remove any sap or debris on the skin. Dry with a clean towel before cutting or cooking.

If fruit oozes sap upon cutting, a piece of cardboard placed over the cutting board keeps it clean. Utensils resist sticky sap when sprayed with a non-stick oil or rubbed with cooking oil. Sap that sticks to kitchen equipment can be removed with oil and a scrub brush followed by washing with dish soap in hot water.

COOKING

STEAMING

The fruit is commonly quartered lengthwise (parallel to the core), after which the core can easily be cut away. The skin, which is edible, can be removed before steaming, left on for consumption, or removed after steaming (which is easiest).

Steam until the flesh is tender and can be easily pierced with a fork. Steaming time varies depending on the size of the steamer and how large the pieces are. Breadfruit can also be boiled. It will absorb more water when boiled than when steamed, which is desirable for certain varieties and recipes, and undesirable for others. Avoid overcooking.

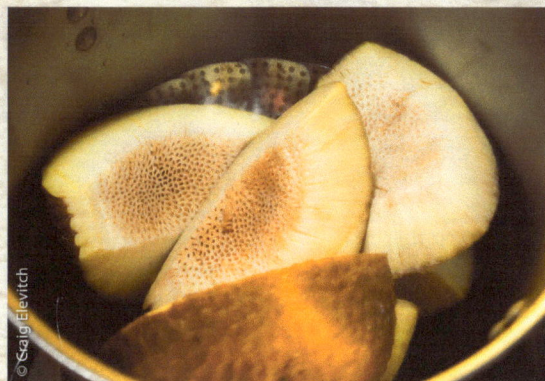

Steaming is a great way to cook breadfruit to eat alone or in dishes. Do not overcook or breadfruit will become mushy and waterlogged!

FRYING

Breadfruit can be pan- or deep-fried, much like potato. If peeled fruit is desired, blanching raw fruit before peeling helps loosen the skin from flesh. A variety of oils complement the taste of breadfruit, including coconut and olive oils. For deep-frying, vegetable oil (such as canola) is recommended. Make sure the oil is hot (355°F or 180°C) before dropping in fruit. Sometimes the fruit is partially steamed or boiled before frying.

BAKING IN OVEN

Oven baking breadfruit results in a tender flesh and a slightly roasted flavor. To bake, rinse the skin, cut in half and place cut side down on an oiled baking sheet or in a shallow baking pan with ½–¾ inch (1–2 cm) of water. Fruit can also be cooked whole wrapped in aluminum foil to keep the flesh moist. Bake at 375–400°F (190–205°C) for one hour or until the fruit can be easily pierced with a fork. Cooking time varies depending on the size of the fruit.

FIRE IT UP!

Hawaiians and other Pacific Islanders traditionally cook breadfruit in underground ovens called imu (Hawaiian) or above ground in umu (Polynesia) or uhmw (Micronesia). It can also be roasted over an open fire. All of these methods impart a wonderful smoky flavor to the fruit. After peeling off the skin, the fruit can be eaten as it is, or as an ingredient in other traditional dishes.

Breadfruit fries are delicious!

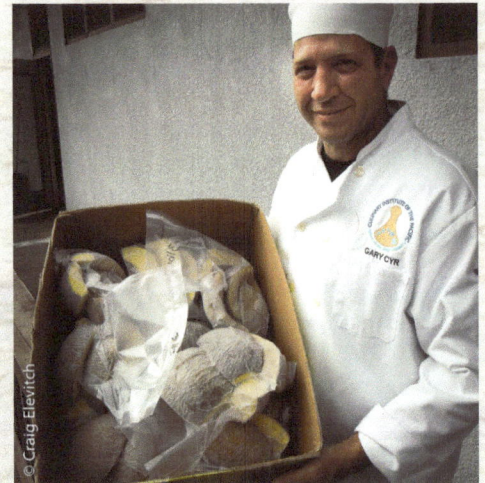

FREEZING COOKED BREADFRUIT

Steamed, cooked pieces should be completely cooled to room temperature (important to avoid freezer burn) and then frozen. When using a freezer-grade plastic bag, quality will be retained for up to a year. Thawed breadfruit processed in this way holds its texture and flavor very well. Boiling is not recommended prior to freezing, as it results in too much water absorption and freezer burn. Note that when frozen raw, the fruit has an unpleasant "sappy" flavor when thawed. However, fully ripe raw fruit freezes well.

Frozen breadfruit should be defrosted in the refrigerator. After thawing, lightly steaming it before use will restore the original texture.

MAKE A DELICIOUS DISH

Breadfruit is delicious all on its own, with just a little butter and salt, or dipped in sauces. Use breadfruit instead of potato in curries, soups, patties, stews, mashed, and salads—it is truly versatile. Find recipes in the *Ho'oulu ka 'Ulu Cookbook* available for purchase at www.breadfruit.info or download free recipes at www.breadfruit.org.

Steamed breadfruit retains its original flavor and texture for up to a year when kept in the freezer.

Left to right: Sam Choy's seafood 'ulu salad, 'ulu chips, Pono Pies' panini and chocolate pies, seafood chowder, and yellow curry.

This publication was produced with funds from the State of Hawai'i Department of Agriculture.

Breadfruit Institute
National Tropical Botanical Garden
3530 Papalina Road
Kalaheo, Kauai, Hawaii USA 96741
Email: breadfruitinstitute@ntbg.org
www.breadfruit.org

Hawai'i Homegrown Food Network
P.O. Box 5, Holualoa, Hawaii, USA 96725
Email: hooulu@hawaiihomegrown.net
www.hawaiihomegrown.net, www.breadfruit.info

APPENDIX 2: BREADFRUIT NUTRITIONAL VALUE AND VERSATILITY

Breadfruit is high in complex carbohydrates, low in fat, and cholesterol and gluten free. It has a moderate glycemic index (blood sugar shock) compared to white potato, white rice, white bread, and taro.

The nutrient compositions of breadfruit (average of the Hawaiian 'Ulu, Ma'afala, and Meinpadahk), white rice, and white potato with the skin, are shown in Table 1. Just 100 g of breadfruit (approximately ½ cup) provides 25% of the RDA for fiber, and 5–10% of the RDA for protein, magnesium, potassium, phosphorus, thiamine (B_1), and niacin (B_3). Breadfruit also provides some carotenoids, such as β-carotene and lutein, which are not present in white rice or white potato.

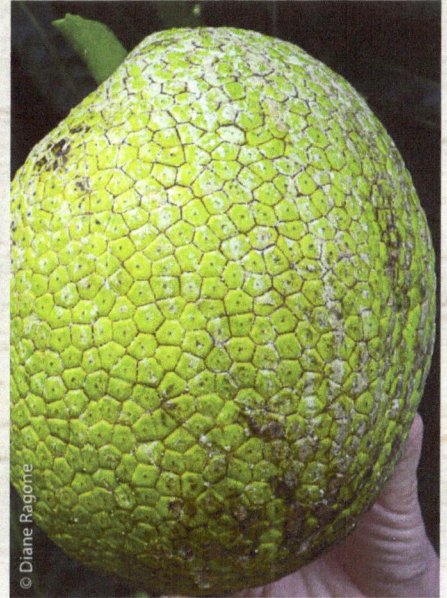

Mature fruit of three varieties. Left to right: Ma'afala, Hawaiian 'Ulu, and Meinpadahk.

Table 1. Nutritional comparison (per 100 g serving)

	Breadfruit*	White potato†	White rice†
Protein (g)	4.0	1.7	2.4
Carbohydrate (g)	31.9	15.7	28.6
Fiber (g)	5.4	2.4	0.3
Phosphorus (mg)	43.1	62.0	37.0
Potassium (mg)	376.7	407.0	29.0
Calcium (mg)	16.8	9.0	3.0
Magnesium (mg)	34.3	21.0	13.0
Sodium (mg)	19.4	16.0	0.0
Iron (mg)	0.5	0.5	0.20
Zinc (mg)	0.1	0.29	0.42
Vitamin C (mg)	2.4	9.1	0.0
Thiamin (mg)	0.1	0.07	0.02
Riboflavin (mg)	0.0	0.03	0.016
Niacin (mg)	0.9	1.06	0.40
Vitamin A (µg)	1.4	0.0	0.0
Lutein (µg)	96.3	0	0
β-Carotene (µg)	15.1	0	0

* Average of three varieties Ma'afala, Hawaiian 'Ulu, and Meinpadahk.
† Data for white potato with skin, medium-grain, cooked, unenriched white rice from: U.S. Department of Agriculture, Agricultural Research Service. 2013. USDA National Nutrient Database for Standard Reference, Release 26. Nutrient Data Laboratory Home Page. www.ars.usda.gov/ba/bhnrc/ndl

Table 2. Relative nutritional value of breadfruit, white potato, and white rice.

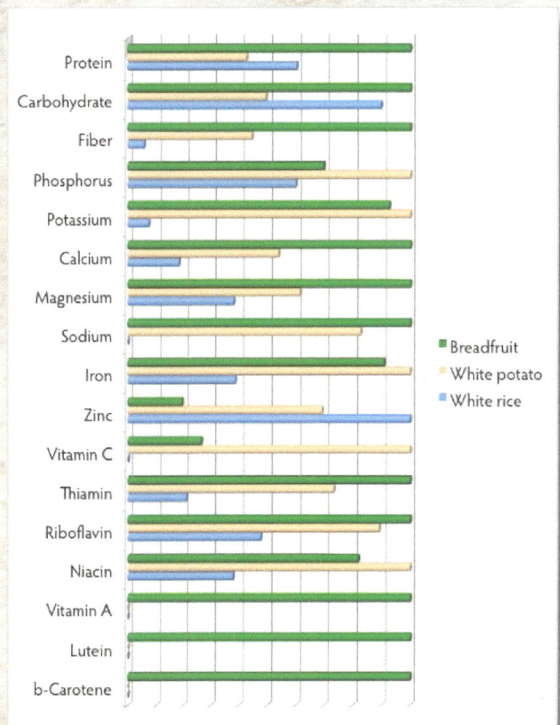

Table 3. Average fruit weight and edible portion for three varieties of breadfruit.

	Whole Fruit Weight	Edible Portion (no peel & core)
Hawaiian 'Ulu	1973 g (4.4 lb)	1734 g (3.8 lb)
Ma'afala	789 g (1.7 lb)	650 g (1.4 lb)
Meinpadahk	1079 g (2.4 lb)	907 g (2.0 lb)

Breadfruit is an extremely versatile fruit that can be prepared and eaten at all stages of development and maturity. Mature fruit is the most desirable to use for most dishes, due to its potato-like texture. There are many ways to prepare mature breadfruit: steamed, boiled, fried, baked, or cooked in traditional ways in a fire. Then it can be used in a variety of dishes such as casseroles, fritters, croquettes, pancakes, breads, curries, stews, chowders, salads and many other dishes. It can also be mashed and made into dips, like hummus, or vegetarian burgers or pâté.

Popular breadfruit dishes in Hawai'i include: salad (like potato salad), curry, cooked in coconut cream, chips, chowder, nachos, and with corned beef.

When breadfruit ripens it becomes soft and creamy and sweet. At this stage it can be eaten raw or used to make beverages, baked goods, desserts like flan, and other sweet dishes.

Immature green fruit, from golf ball size to almost full size, can be cooked entire, or cut into thin slices or chunks and boiled until tender. Once cooked, they can be eaten with dips, used in salads, and marinated, or pickled. The flavor and texture resembles artichoke heart.

Traditional methods of cooking 'ulu are roasting directly on a fire until the skin blackened and the flesh was tender, baking in the imu (underground oven), and pounding into a doughy consistency (for poi or other uses). A modern twist involves putting cooked 'ulu from the imu or boiled/steamed, through a food grinder (e.g. Champion brand), adding a little bit of coconut oil to give it a nice texture. This type of preparation can be used like dough, rolled out for pasta, pizza, or tamales.

Another way to use breadfruit is to peel and core the raw fruit, shred or slice it into thin pieces, then dry and grind into a meal or flour. The coarse meal can substitute for panko or breadcrumbs. Since the flour is gluten free, it will not rise or have the elasticity of wheat flour, but can be used like other gluten-free flours.

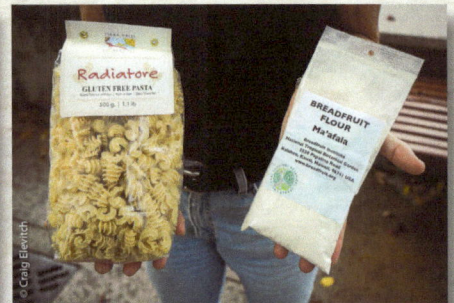

Clockwise from top left: Ready-to-eat steamed quarters; Removing blackened skin from fire-roasted breadfruit; Breadfruit pasta and flour; Pono Pies panini breadfruit pie; Breadfruit and chicken yellow curry; Breadfruit salad with local vegetables.

This publication was produced with funds from the State of Hawai'i Department of Agriculture.

Department of Agriculture STATE OF HAWAII

Breadfruit Institute
National Tropical Botanical Garden
3530 Papalina Road
Kalaheo, Kauai, Hawaii USA 96741
Email: breadfruitinstitute@ntbg.org
www.breadfruit.org

NATIONAL TROPICAL BOTANICAL GARDEN · BREADFRUIT INSTITUTE

Hawai'i Homegrown Food Network
P.O. Box 5, Holualoa, Hawaii, USA 96725
Email: hooulu@hawaiihomegrown.net
www.hawaiihomegrown.net, www.breadfruit.info

HAWAI'I HOMEGROWN® FOOD NETWORK

Breadfruit Variety—Ma'afala

This popular variety originated in Samoa and Tonga and has been grown in Hawai'i for decades. Ma'afala is a fast-growing tree that tends to be shorter, with a more compact form than most breadfruit varieties. Since 2009, thousands of Ma'afala trees propagated using micropropagation methods have been planted throughout Hawai'i and they are beginning to bear fruit as early as 2½–3 years after planting.

The fruit is oval. At maturity, brownish cracking (or scabbing) develops on and around the individual sections of the skin and a slight separation between the sections indicates maturity, along with the skin turning a greenish-yellow color and becoming relatively smooth. The pale yellow flesh may occasionally contain 1 or 2 small seeds. This variety has one of the smallest fruit with an average weight of 790 g (1.7 lb) and an edible portion (peel and core removed) of 650 g (1.4 lb).

Mature fruit of Ma'afala: Look for greenish-yellow skin, a smooth surface, and brownish cracking between the surface segments. The flesh inside is firm and creamy white or pale yellow in color.

Ma'afala is intermediate in texture, firmness, and cooking time compared to the Hawaiian 'Ulu and Micronesian varieties such as Meinpadahk. This makes it a versatile choice for a wider array of recipes. The flesh is moister and tenderer than 'Ulu when baked or roasted, yet maintains its texture and firmness if desired for a particular recipe, such as 'ulu salad, and can also be easily mashed for dishes such as patties or croquettes.

Young Ma'afala trees may have smaller than average size fruit during the first 2–3 years after they begin producing, and fruit size and abundance increases as the tree matures. Fruit size can vary with tree location and management practices. Fruit drop may occur on young trees, or ones that experience environmental stress such as drought, or lack of essential micronutrients.

Breadfruit salad made with local vegetables.

A 5-year-old Ma'afala tree showing compact form.

This publication was produced with funds from the State of Hawai'i Department of Agriculture.
Department of Agriculture STATE OF HAWAII

Breadfruit Institute
National Tropical Botanical Garden
3530 Papalina Road
Kalaheo, Kauai, Hawaii USA 96741
Email: breadfruitinstitute@ntbg.org
www.breadfruit.org

Hawai'i Homegrown Food Network
P.O. Box 5, Holualoa, Hawaii, USA 96725
Email: hooulu@hawaiihomegrown.net
www.hawaiihomegrown.net, www.breadfruit.info

Breadfruit Variety—'Ulu

The 'Ulu variety is a typical seedless, dense, starchy Polynesian breadfruit that was brought to Hawai'i from Tahiti by the original Hawaiians. It is believed that 'Ulu arrived 500–700 years ago, possibly earlier. 'Ulu was widely grown in Hawai'i, with vast managed groves in Kona and Puna on Hawai'i Island and large plantings elsewhere throughout the islands.

The fruit is oval to round, with a light green skin color and slightly rough skin. Mature and ready to use fruit typically has pronounced brownish cracking (scabbing) on and around the individual sections on the skin, and a slight separation between the sections, combined with a crust of dried drops of sap. The flesh is white to cream colored and seedless. The fruit is large, with an average weight of about 2 kg (4.4 lb) and an edible portion (peel and core removed) of 1.7 kg (3.8 lb).

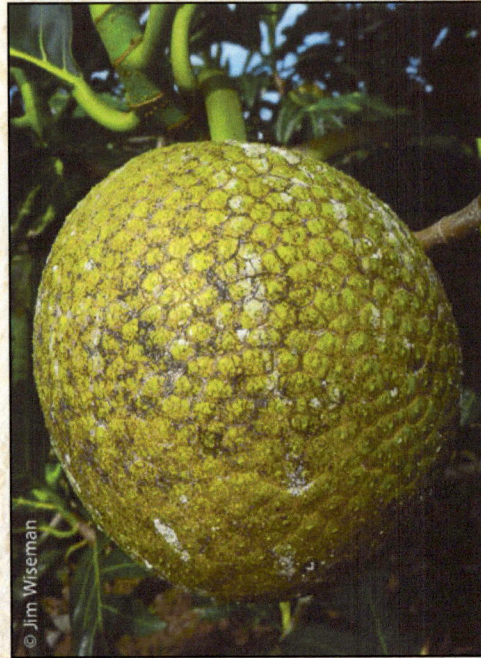

Mature fruit of 'Ulu: Look for greenish-yellow skin, a smooth surface, and brownish cracking between the surface segments. A crust of dried sap is also typical. The flesh inside is firm and creamy white or pale yellow in color.

'Ulu has denser, firmer, and starchier texture compared with Ma'afala and Meinpadahk, and consequently takes longer to cook and tends to be on the dry side when roasted or baked. The solid, dense texture makes it ideal for dishes that require a firm slice, such as au gratin dishes, fries, or chips. 'Ulu can be steamed or boiled, which adds moisture. The longer it is cooked, the more tender and softer the flesh becomes, so it can be cooked to a texture desired for a given dish.

The Hawaiian 'Ulu fruit can vary in fruit size, shape, and production season depending on where the tree is growing, but fruit quality, texture and cooking qualities remain constant.

Breadfruit seafood chowder made with fish, shrimp, broth, taro leaves and other vegetables

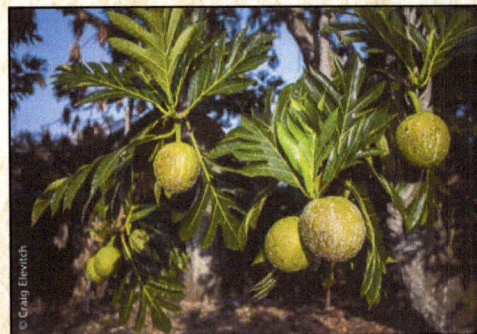

Hawaiian 'Ulu fruit size and shape can vary, but eating qualities remain constant

This publication was produced with funds from the State of Hawai'i Department of Agriculture.

Department of Agriculture STATE OF HAWAII

Breadfruit Institute
National Tropical Botanical Garden
3530 Papalina Road
Kalaheo, Kauai, Hawaii USA 96741
Email: breadfruitinstitute@ntbg.org
www.breadfruit.org

Hawai'i Homegrown Food Network
P.O. Box 5, Holualoa, Hawaii, USA 96725
Email: hooulu@hawaiihomegrown.net
www.hawaiihomegrown.net, www.breadfruit.info

Breadfruit Variety—Meinpadahk

This variety is a natural hybrid between two species, breadfruit (*Artocarpus altilis*) and dugdug (*A. mariannensis*). It is grown in the Federated States of Micronesia, the Marshall Islands, Kiribati and elsewhere in Micronesia. It does well in sandy soils of atolls and coastal regions, but it also thrives in volcanic and other soils. Meinpadahk and other Micronesian varieties were brought to Hawai'i beginning in the late 1800s.

The fruit is oval to oblong, with a distinctive bumpy, light green waxy or shiny skin. The individual sections of the skin are pebbly in appearance. The skin does not change color or develop crusts of sap or scabbing when mature, so proper harvest can be challenging. Maturity is indicated by the sections beginning to separate from each other and a subtle change in color to greenish-yellow. The pale to deep yellow flesh is seedless. This variety has an average weight of 1080 g (2.4 lb) and an edible portion of 900 g (2 lb).

Mature fruit of Meinpadahk: Maturity is indicated by the sections beginning to separate from each other and a subtle change in color to greenish-yellow. The flesh has a soft, creamy texture when cooked.

The flesh of Micronesian varieties like Meinpadahk is less solid and dense than 'Ulu or Ma'afala and is relatively lightweight for its size. It has a soft, creamy texture when cooked and is easily mashed or puréed. The fruit is very tender and moist when baked or roasted, and can be quickly steamed to a desired texture. Boiling tends to waterlog the flesh. Use this variety for many dishes that require a soft, delicate fruit. A combination of 2 or 3 varieties in a breadfruit salad or casserole will provide a pleasing range of textures from soft to firm.

Meinpadahk is a heavy producer and may abort or drop many of its fruits before they reach full size or maturity.

Gratin layered with Meinpadahk and 'Ulu

Meinpadahk tree loaded with fruit

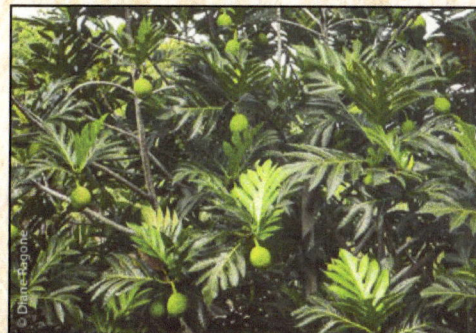

This publication was produced with funds from the State of Hawai'i Department of Agriculture.

Department of Agriculture STATE OF HAWAII

Breadfruit Institute
National Tropical Botanical Garden
3530 Papalina Road
Kalaheo, Kauai, Hawaii USA 96741
Email: breadfruitinstitute@ntbg.org
www.breadfruit.org

Hawai'i Homegrown Food Network
P.O. Box 5, Holualoa, Hawaii, USA 96725
Email: hooulu@hawaiihomegrown.net
www.hawaiihomegrown.net, www.breadfruit.info

HAWAI'I HOMEGROWN FOOD NETWORK

HO'OULU KA 'ULU
Revitalizing Breadfruit

NOTES

www.ingramcontent.com/pod-product-compliance
Lightning Source LLC
Chambersburg PA
CBHW060824090426

42738CB00003B/104